DARK NLP

Understanding and Using the Secret NLP Methods of Manipulation in Conversational Manipulation. Become an Expert in Manipulating People's Minds with Dark Methods
(2022 Guide for Beginners)

Joey Lowe

Contents

INTRODUCTION...7

What exactly is NLP?...8

NLP's History 9

The NLP Techniques..10

Update on Physiology 12

Visualization..13

Taking Away the Right to Say No 14

CHAPTER 1...15

WHAT EXACTLY IS NLP...15

A Short History...15

NLP's Foundations 17

Rapport..18

Sensory Perception 19

Thinking about the Endgame...20

Behaviour Flexibility..21

Knowledge Application..24

NLP AS A MANIPULATION TOOL.......................................28

NLP Techniques for Mind Control in the Media and Political Cults 32

Areas Where Mass Mind Manipulation Occurs 34

Governments and the news media 34

Marketing and advertising 38

CHAPTER 3..40

NLP TECHNIQUES..40

Dissociation 40

Content Reframing 41

Pacing in the Future..44

Swish 46

CHAPTER 4..47

NLP AND THE HUMAN BRAIN..47

NLP Is a Difficult Strategy 47

As a Strategic Business Tool, NLP.....................................50

Main Industries Where NLP Has a Significant Impact ..51

An Effective Strategy 52

1. Identify Your Target Audience 53

2. Outcomes 54

3. Describe Your Current Experience 54

4. Bring about a new experience 56

5. Maintain Your Integrity 57

CHAPTER 5 60

TIPS FOR APPLYING NLP 60

Tip 1: The Why Question 60

Tip 2: Your behaviour is almost never incorrect 61

Tip 3: Manage Your Emotions 61

Tip 4: Your Point of View 62

Tip 5: Accepting Compliments 62

Tip 6: Speaking to Yourself 63

Tip 7: When Issues Arise 64

Tip 8: It Doesn't Matter What Has Happened in the past.
.... 64

Tip 9: Remember to Breathe 65

CHAPTER 6 66

PRESUPPOSITIONS IN NLP 66

Replicating Successful Patterns 67

Primary Representational Systems (PRS) 69

Proxemics 72

Success Patterns 73

Levels of Neurology 74

CHAPTER 7 75

COMMUNICATION AND NLP 75

What Exactly Is NLP Communication? 77

Laws of NLP Communication 78

Communication Channels for NLP......................79

Communication Styles in NLP............................81

Verbal Communication Using NLP 81

Nonverbal Communication (NLP) 82

Visual Communication Using NLP 83

Language of the Body...83

What Is the Difference Between Informing and Communicating?...84

Recognize Body Language..................................85

Body Language Messages of Satisfaction 86

The rejection messages show the opposite.........87

Tension Discharges in Body Language................87

CHAPTER 8...89

NLP IN BUSINESS...89

....89

Work to Get Results 90

Understand and Be Conscious of Your Senses.................92

Change Your Behavior to Ensure a Successful Outcome

....93

Take Initiative...94

Using NLP to Increase Sales.......................................97

CHAPTER 9...99

NLP IN RELATIONSHIPS...99

CONCLUSION..109

INTRODUCTION

Neuro-Linguistic Programming, or NLP, is a vital tool for mind control. NLP tactics are used by news anchors and others on TV and cable news, as well as by leaders, trainers, and other media celebrities, and by those who act to control you. However, most NLP goals are unaware that they are under mind stimulation command, which is one of the aspects that contributes to the effectiveness of this technique. NLP employs various techniques to induce a trance-like condition in humans, making them receptive to ideas. The tools used in the Neuro-Linguistic Programming NLP are a type of hypnosis. Many of those approaches have been utilized for years by manipulators and others involved in mind manipulation.

What exactly is NLP?

Neuro-Linguistic Programming (NLP) is a type of mind control created in the 1970s. This was when many scholars were working with novel behavioural and psychological theories, as you will see as we delve into its history. Approaches like NLP looked to use knowledge and abilities that had been accumulated both as a result of men who had used hypnosis and mind control in the past and the new areas of social understanding that were disclosed by the hard natural and social sciences.

When we discussed the history of mind control, we discussed guys like Rasputin, who appeared to use dark and secretive skills that it was difficult for others to grasp how they sought to do what they did. Looking at Rasputin's photographs, his eyes are the most surprising feature. He appears to be looking out of the frame, almost as if he is sharing your space with you. Rasputin's manipulation and control techniques were unknown at the time, but it appears that components of what we'd term NLP mind control can be seen in some of his approaches today.

NLP mind manipulation practitioners utilize effective communication as a method to induce relationships in their aim. Despite the fact that NLP guides are more focused on tactics and less on psychology, this type of strategy instils in a human the desire to have an emotional and psychological bond with everyone. Intense eye contact, when paired with other words, gestures, or other signs, can make someone vulnerable to mind control or even put them in a trance. Many people nowadays employ NLP tactics to achieve their aims, even if the purpose is to sell you something for a small profit.

NLP's History

Neuro-Linguistic Programming was evolved in the 1970s by Richard Bandler and John Grinder, two Californians with backgrounds in psychology and linguistics. The most striking element of NLP is that it combines research from numerous fields with a deep understanding of the human condition and motives. The customs of Fritz Perls, Milton Erickson, and Virginia Satir are the most relevant to NLP.

Milton Erickson is a name that has had a significant psychological and hypnotic impact. His skills were allegedly adopted by a variety of people, including well-known public speakers such as Tony Robbins. Ericksonian methods are still employed in psychotherapy, but NLP hypnotists and therapists have adopted them because they make the person more observant and susceptible to influence and regulation.

Ericksonian technologies are intended to obtain access to the collective unconscious, which NLP accomplished in a spectacular fashion. The NLP gained popularity in the 1980s and 1990s.

The NLP Techniques

The NLP tactics are so innovative that most people who are new to NLP go beneath the radar. Neuro-Linguistic training methods have been claimed by people such as former US President Barack Obama, whose words are presented as examples of permissive speech hypnosis, an NLP approach. As previously said, NLP technologies are derived from an understanding of how the mind works, what motivates human behaviour, how humans create relationships with one another, and how humans generally communicate and act.

Manipulators and narcissists pay attention to the cues that indicate your psychological reaction or your objectives and intents. NLP practitioners are also paying attention to you, attempting to figure out how to develop the connection bond, looking for clues on how you think, and looking for opportunities to induce hypnosis. Here is a list of many of the things that an NLP practitioner looks for:

Describe how your brain grows through the use of eye movements. Defines how your brain saves facts with the help of eye movements. Determine which point of view dominates your mind. Determine which side of the brain has the upper hand. Identify when you lie.

Neuro-Linguistic Coding is a subset of dark psychology that is very close to the surface in terms of common knowledge, as many people utilize it, yet it is still a potent weapon for mind control. Later on, we'll see how those motivated to protect themselves can deviate from their training.

Update on Physiology

Shaking up the physical surroundings might often be just what you need to utilize NLP to persuade or appraise someone else. Perhaps something is attempting to obstruct your path during the chat. To establish a more congenial atmosphere, consider moving alongside the person you're talking to. If you feel the conversation isn't progressing as you'd like, take a break in the restroom and give the person some alone time.

If you're on your way back from the restroom and everything is still the same, say you turn the place up. You can take a drive or relax on the patio. However, you are not required to drive at excessive speeds. Changing your body position or the way you sit may be enough to reengage the other person.

Visualization

For some people, visualization is an effective technique to achieve their goals. Numerous factors may appear out of control, but if you simply imagine what you want, you'll be surprised at how much you can accomplish.

Something can begin by talking itself into existence. If you want to move to Los Angeles, start fantasizing about becoming an actor. Don't tell anyone; you just have to do it at some point. Say you're going to do it, and you'll be shocked at how far you can influence yourself toward those goals.

If necessary, write it down as well. It's more of a self-persuasion tactic than one you'd use on someone else, and it also helps to talk and write about the goals and wishes you want to see realized.

Taking Away the Right to Say No

We touched on this briefly earlier, but removing another person's ability to say no is an NLP tactic used for persuasive communication. Rather than saying, "Would you like to come out for dinner tonight?" "Where are we going to eat tonight?" inquired someone. You did not give them the choice of declining. In any case, they may claim they can't, but you can still choose to eliminate the possibility.

Rather than asking, "Can I have one?" "How many may I have?" you ask. Most people will not even notice that their ability to refuse you has been diminished.

CHAPTER 1
WHAT EXACTLY IS NLP

A Short History

In the 1970s, John Grinder and Richard Bandler, two of the founders of Neurolinguistic Programming, attempted to develop explicit models of human greatness. The Structure of Magic, their first collaboration, identified the behavioural and verbal patterns of two colleagues, Virginia Satir and Fritz Perls. Their next cooperation, patterns of Hypnotic Techniques of Milton H. Erickson, looked at Erickson's behaviour and linguistic patterns as a recognized psychiatrist.

When Bandler, a warehouse assistant at Science and Behavioral Books, and Frank Pucelik, a Vietnam War veteran, met, they agreed to help one other reconstruct their lives. They reproduced the approaches stated in the transcripts and tapes, most notably those of Fritz Perls, the pioneer of Gestalt Therapy, using Bandler's link to a publishing company. Initially, their primary goal was to better their lives.

Bandler and Pucelik began practising Gestalt Therapy with a group at the University of California, Santa Cruz, after encountering Perls' writing (UCSC). Soon after, they were joined by John Grinder, a young linguistics professor at UCSC. Grinder's observations and queries marked the start of a long and fruitful collaboration between the three, which resulted in the development of neuro-linguistic programming. They used their joint abilities and ingenuity to evaluate and model Perls' and Virginia Satir's works, as well as the outcomes of Virginia Satir, the mother of family therapy. They aimed to replicate Perls and Satir's research by determining the reasons behind their success. They were later introduced to Milton Erickson's works, a psychiatrist who specialized in medical hypnosis and family therapy.

Grinder and Bandler contributed to and standardized their methodologies and conclusions from their early works, eventually dubbing it "Neurolinguistic Programming." They wanted to represent the connection between the brain, body, and language.

Professionals have polished NLP over the years, generating new abilities and tools for communication and change. By the 1990s, a new generation of NLP had emerged, focusing on themes like identity, mission, and vision. Since the mid-1970s, NLP has spread over the world and improved many people's lives, proving notably beneficial in sales, counselling and psychotherapy, law, management, creative arts, health, and education.

NLP's Foundations

The NLP objectives will be housed in these four pillars. You will employ any of the tactics of one or more of these methods, altering your perception of them. The four pillars are rapport, sensory awareness, outcome thinking, and behavioural flexibility.

Rapport

If you plan on applying NLP with others, rapport is one of the essential tools you will require. If you are planning to use NLP on someone else, you must first build a connection with them. This is really just acknowledging that you and the other person have a mutually beneficial relationship—you both get along, agree with each other, and like each other. If you intend to use NLP on someone else, you must be eager and ready to build a relationship with them to open up that communication channel between yourself and those other people. This is potent, and you will need it—without it, you will not be able to have the desired effect.

Finally, depending on their body language, you can discern if you have this rapport with someone else. Is it possible that they are imitating your body language? Then you most likely have some sort of relationship with them. We tend to replicate the habits of persons we like or trust frequently. If you like or trust someone, you will be encouraged to copy them simply because mirror neurons—areas in your brain that activate when they see someone else doing something—are activated.

You can also actively mirror someone else's behaviours in an attempt to get them to reflect you back—you can do this by looking for subtle body language and attempting to copy it, such as taking a drink almost immediately after they do if you are sitting together at a restaurant, or by shifting your position every time they do.

Sensory Perception

Finally, when attempting to apply NLP, you must be fully aware of everything that is going on. You must be mindful of your surroundings, whether you are using it on yourself or attempting to use it on someone else. This means you must be able to recognize nonverbal clues in yourself and others. You must be able to detect when your emotions are communicating something or when your body language is betraying the feelings that you are experiencing at the time. When you are fully aware of this, you begin to gain a wealth of additional information into the scenario. You can tell, for example, that your body language indicates that you are anxious, so you pause to investigate what is causing you to be nervous around you. This simple method helps you determine what is going on with you, why it is happening, and how it is happening.

Thinking about the Endgame

Outcome thinking refers to your capacity to identify a goal that you want to see accomplished. If you wish to change your mental processes to fit better what you believe they should be, you must be willing and able to establish some form of goal for them. Finally, it is only by having a well-thought-out objective that you will be able to begin to create the changes in your life that you are hoping for or desperate to see. This pillar serves as a type of guide for you—you can't be confident you'll be able to change in the ways you want to change if you don't identify what you're changing. However, after you've decided on a goal, you may start focusing on it. You may begin by directing both your body and mind to achieve it, and you can go through the effort of ensuring that it happens in the way that you want it to happen at the end of the day. You will be aware of your objectives and, as a result, will understand how to keep working toward them.

Behaviour Flexibility

Finally, the final NLP foundation is behavioural flexibility. Recognizing that what you are doing is not always working for you, and then knowing that it is critical for you to adjust your activities in order to find a solution to make things work. You will be able to recognize when it is time to abandon what you have tried in favour of other approaches that may work better for you.

When you establish this level of adaptability, you are accomplishing two things. To begin, you are assuring that you can locate a way that works to assist you in reaching your goal. This is a critical point—you want to ensure that you can get your own goals at the end of the day. However, that is not the only thing that occurs in this case. You'll also be promoting resiliency. You know that something did not go as planned and can therefore be flexible about it.

Keep in mind that NLP is all about positivism. It's all about recognizing that while you can't always control the outcome, you can control how you react to it. Being adaptable in your behaviour entails doing precisely that—recognizing that you tried something that did not work, and as a result, they may identify exactly how they need to change to have the best possible chance of success.

With this engaging graphic, authors Romilla Ready and Kate Burton show how the four pillars might be applied in your daily life.

Assume you purchased new software to assist you in keeping track of all your friends' and clients' names, addresses, phone numbers, and other critical information. After acquiring and installing the software, you realize that it does not function properly due to a coding error.

You contact the customer care department of the software firm, and they are unpleasant and useless. At this stage, you must use your relationship-building talents to get the customer service manager to listen to your problems. You'd need to improve your sensory awareness by paying close attention, controlling your emotions, and deciding on the best reaction. You must communicate your desired outcome to the customer care manager; do you want a refund or a replacement? Finally, your behaviour must be adaptable enough to accept alternative products if the targeted outcome is not feasible.

That is how NLP assists you in becoming a better communicator and achieving your goals without a lot of stress or aggravation.

Knowledge Application

Modelling is predicated on several critical assumptions. The first is that our sensory systems, which we employ to represent our worlds, process experience. In other words, for one person, working as a janitor is a nightmare, while for another, it is a dream come true. To one person, having money and a solid job is unsatisfying; to another, this life is lovely and is supplemented by other enjoyable pursuits.

Modelling assumes that people observe the environment through their senses and then store that knowledge in their minds. When this information is stored, it produces memories, which are subsequently linked to sights, sounds, smells, textures, and so on. Many of these mental images are unconscious. Consider any day-to-day activity. When you make coffee, tie your shoes, drive to work, brush your teeth, or move around your house, your brain access memories that allow you to behave appropriately.

In NLP, when we model a 'template,' we essentially adopt the exemplar's behaviours, language, techniques, and beliefs to mimic success's behavioural outcome. Of course, modelling is not limited to 'success' in the classic business or moneymaking sense. It can also have an impact on a wide variety of human learning. Finally, these newly acquired attitudes, cognitive patterns, emotional responses, and behavioural consequences treat a wide range of problems and challenges. Fears and phobias, mood disorders such as depression, habit disorders such as obsession and compulsion, psychosomatic illnesses (thinking you're unwell when you're not), bodily maladies, and learning disabilities are examples of such issues.

Simply put, if we use NLP appropriately, it has the power to change everything in our lives. The passion for excellent programming is evident, whether in the company or personal life.

NLP can help with personal success in the following ways:

- Improve your comprehension of thoughts, emotions, and behaviours.

- Boost and Maintain Motivation

- Streamline Money, Career, Health, Relationships, and Family Values

- Attract Complementary Individuals

- Reduce or eliminate maladaptive thoughts and behaviours. Release Maladaptive Elements from the Past

- Determine Outcomes and Goals Approaching Goals Proactively Maintain High-Quality Relationships Reduce or Apply Harmful Stress

- Obtaining Peak Physical and Mental Health Create a Positive Self-Image

- Establish Immediate Relationship

NLP can help with job/career/work success by:

- Goals must be set and achieved to reduce barriers.

- Get Rid of Unwanted Behaviors

- Encourage Long-Term Partnerships Reduce Cultural and Contextual Restrictions Improve Communication

- Boost Negotiation Skills Maximize Conflict Resolution Increase Sales

- Boost Productivity by Improving Workplace Synergy

NLP AS A MANIPULATION TOOL

Your goals are the only North Star in a dark and lonely ocean. The single element distinguishes NLP from manipulation by acting as a valuable tool for remembering the true objective of employing NLP. Studies demonstrate that when you are intrinsically aware of your goals, even when you aren't actively thinking about them, your brain works discreetly towards accomplishing them. When you let your mind wander freely, finding connections at random, this is referred to as "diffused thinking."

It is a procedure that uses all regions of the brain to solve issues and understand challenging concepts. The true motivation can remain undisturbed, deep in your subconscious, while your brain works around it, devising strategies and plans to achieve it. NLP is a collection of abilities that allows you to control your own conscious and unconscious mind as the user. However, this does not rule out the possibility of NLP being successful if the user's motives are immoral. It is conceivable to instil those habits that have historically been practised by unpleasant personalities such as criminals and terrorists.

As a result, the patient can be moulded into the next revolutionary terrorist, ushering in a new period and completely reinventing modern violence as we know it. This is one of the more extreme examples. More subtle influence, which may not make headlines or morning news, can be just as lethal.

Consider the following hypothetical scenario with two rival legal firms competing for the same large client. Law firm 'A' intends to influence the client's decision by casting a negative light on their competing law practice. This is accomplished by employing a programmer to sit in on Law Firm 'B's top attorney's regular therapy sessions and slowly change the patient's image of their connection with their spouse, planting subconscious indications of difficulties in the relationship that do not exist. With or without NLP, this strategy would fall under the category of courtroom manipulation. Beggars' emotional manipulation is another example of manipulation that your brain does not often identify because humans are sympathetic creatures. Though there are some 'honest' beggars who are genuinely homeless and trying to survive, the vast majority of individuals whose trade is begging are not.

It's very prevalent in South Asia, and the manipulators usually wear spotty clothes and have dirty faces. They utilize words and acts to manipulate people's emotions in order to persuade them that they require money. Many go so far as to employ youngsters for the day simply to rub it in. The manipulation is done so well that they are great at it whether they are trained in NLP techniques or not. NLP programmers hired to hold regular seminars at businesses (such as our fictional law firms) utilize it to enhance employee enthusiasm and push them to learn.

Extraordinary success has been associated with new skill sets to boost worker productivity and employee attitude. It is a method that has yielded positive results. Similarly, much as it is used in business to motivate employees, door-to-door salespeople often use it to sell as many things as possible and earn more significant commissions. Personal programmers assist their clients in repairing connections with friends and family members and rectifying and resolving issues. NLP is also used in the treatment of mental diseases such as PTSD, GAD, phobias, anxiety, paranoia, and even substance abuse.

There are other such cases where NLP is used for good or ill, but the overriding truth is that NLP is not guilty. There are users and abusers of this approach, as with any other technique or commodity. The thing being (ab)used is not guilty of the (ab)user's crime. NLP abusers with immoral, evil objectives have tarnished Bandler and Grinder's well-intended personal development and psychotherapy technique.

NLP Techniques for Mind Control in the Media and Political Cults

Would the world be a better place if we all had the freedom to make our own decisions? Does our individual decision assist the group as a whole? Because we are unable to do so jointly, others make decisions for us. The concept of "mind control" or "brainwashing" can elicit a variety of emotions in you. Would it be regarded as a breach of your most precious God-given right — free will? Whatever the nature of its application, you may have a slight aversion to the concept or oppose it entirely. Mind-control techniques, like any other instrument, can be utilized for good or exploited for personal advantage at the expense of others.

Mass mind-control comprises covert, sophisticated operations with a considerable impact on our world, with the media taking centre stage and serving as a tool for whoever controls it.

Many of us are oblivious to mind-controlling programs' violent and upsetting nature. However, those who are aware of it may choose to disregard it (perhaps this is another type of mind control and not want to make the conscious effort to use their grey matter). Some are content to let others think, allowing those in power free rein to increase fear and divergence in our world.

It is a fairly typical practice for businesses, governments, and everything in between to mislead you into believing in something you did not consider. People have been in the dark for a long time, unaware that such a thing exists. But, owing to individuals who violated the vow of silence to speak out against the injustice of such issues, you have been forced to open your eyes and minds today.

Sometimes those persons are made to appear rebellious, such as Julian Assange, an Australian editor, publisher, and Wikileaks founder. We think the way we do because we are trained to, thanks to the foundation previously established by the powers that be, and the rest that follows is the logical conclusion. Some dark NLP components are required for the parts of cooperative society to be firmly entrenched. A nation does not face irreversible ruin if turmoil and anarchy break out.

Areas Where Mass Mind Manipulation Occurs

Governments and the news media

Is it possible for a democratically elected government to influence the will of the people? We have watched the establishment of many powerful empires, regimes, and governments, as well as their success in authoritative rule, throughout our world's history. Do democratically elected governments rule? Governments all around the globe have long employed mind control and brainwashing. They use the media as a vehicle to deliver their message.

Politics and the media have forged a strong alliance in this potent art of deception. They target distinct segments of the population to address specific problems that are relevant to them, reframing their thinking. They have the ability to shape the narrative on news channels and in newspapers. They can create and fix nonexistent problems, they can divert attention away from the world's problems, and there will be no one to speak out against them. Frequently, problems are created solely to create a demand for a solution in which the government steps in. Manipulation is at its most effective!

Wag the Dog (1997), a comedy about how the media may distort public opinion, is excellent. This film demonstrates how the media employs pictures and signs (NLP) to divert (manipulate) the public's attention away from problems that may not be relevant to them. It demonstrates the power that the media can exert on the populace. Governments allow regulated substances such as booze, antidepressants, narcotics, nicotine, and prescription medications to be used to control specific groups of people so that they do not respond in ways that disrupt the societal equilibrium.

According to Freedom House President Michael Abramowitz, hired critics and political forecasters of government propaganda have established themselves and have become a global trend. The fear factor is another technique to ensure that the country does not overstep its bounds. You invent a fearsome cause, such as an incurable disease or terrorist agents, and claim to be out on the streets monitoring unethical behaviours and those who assist the criminals. Conspiracy theorists frequently believe that "false-flag" disasters are staged with the help of crisis actors.

JAWS (1975) was one of the greatest films ever created, and it remained a top-grossing film until 1977. During this historical period, little was known about sharks. The film elicited a strong reaction of panic, fear, and terror, causing beachgoers worldwide to avoid even the safest beaches. When the subject of sharks comes up, the media exploits those anxieties.

You are made to be afraid of speaking out in public regarding certain things. You're programmed to be frightened of assisting a stranger because you don't know what his motivation is. Will offering a helpful hand-land you in hot water? You are concerned that your phone calls are being recorded. You must always keep an eye on your back.

Take, for example, North Korea. It is still the most oppressive country on the planet. The government maintains ultimate political control over its society through fear, and its people's activities are closely watched with an iron hand.

In this day and age, the art of persuasion has become a lucrative business, with advertising playing a vital role. You are constantly trained and told what you should eat, what beauty items you should buy, what insurance you should get, what medical procedures you should follow, how you should manage your lifestyle, and where you should spend. When you turn on your television, you are assaulted with adverts attempting to persuade you to purchase a particular product. Marketing is based on manipulative concepts. Because your mind absorbs all that information, the strategies utilized in magazines, billboards, posters, newspapers, free flyers, and television unconsciously tease you. You will develop a desire for the products if you view them enough times.

Marketing and advertising

Most marketers unethically manipulate their target audience in order to create an attachment to the product. Marketers do not only target adults; they also target youngsters. The majority of advertising for child-related products is broadcast on the children's channel or during commercial breaks at a children's movie. As an adult, you are prone to spoiling your children and coming up with novel methods to celebrate events such as Valentine's Day, which has now become a significant commercial event. Marketers plan for such events for weeks in advance.

Beauty pageants, fashion shows, apparel catalogues, and fashion publications depict perfect-looking models and celebrities who promote models with ideal bodies, particularly to teens, giving them the notion that wealth and success are a byproduct of the slim form. As a result, many cases of anorexia and bulimia among teenagers and young adults seek the perfect image at the expense of their health. Marketers use persons who are believed to be gorgeous or handsome and celebrities to sell things and gain considerable profits.

They think that everything can be sold provided it appeals to the consumer and is deemed appealing.

Market manipulation is used for marketing the image by manipulating individuals looking for this perceived picture. Most individuals appreciate the arts, movies, and music as forms of amusement. Nonetheless, the industry and governments exploit them as a sort of diversion, which falls under the heading of manipulation.

The entertainment business is dominated by a small group of people who use thought-provoking topics with hidden messages to tug at your heartstrings, bring tears to your eyes, or frighten you. Movies about doomsday scenarios offer people a sense of the likelihood of something similar happening in the future; once again, you see consumerism at its best as people gather to buy survival gear.

CHAPTER 3

NLP TECHNIQUES

Dissociation

The first thing we're going to look at is a process called dissociation. Have you ever walked into a scenario and just had a horrible feeling about it from the start? Or perhaps there are particular scenarios that will cause you to feel sad or dejected each time you encounter them. Or you can be in a circumstance at work that makes you uneasy, such as having to speak in front of a large group of people.

These events demonstrate the whole gamut of emotions that you might experience, and they frequently appear to be something that you must cope with, ones that are automatic and unstoppable. However, by employing skills from dark NLP and dissociation, you will be able to turn these feelings away and stop them from bothering you.

Content Reframing

Try this strategy if you are feeling low or helpless in a situation. Reframing can inspire you by transforming an unpleasant situation into something helpful.

Let's say you've decided to end a relationship. That may sound terrible at first, but let's rephrase it. What appears to be the benefits of getting single? For starters, you're now reachable to specific potential partners. You have the right to do whatever you want, whenever you want. And you've learned valuable things from your prior relationship that will help you have much better future ones.

All of these are examples of how a situation might be reframed. By redefining the circumstances of the breakup, you offer yourself a new understanding of this.

It's natural to worry or be anxious in planned conditions, but this only adds to the problem. Turning your attention to something else, on the other hand, helps cleanse your thoughts and allows you to make more sensible, even-handed decisions.

Establishing Yourself

The term "centring" comes from the Russian psychologist Ivan Pavlov, who demonstrated it with dogs by constantly circling a bell while the canines ate. He discovered that by ringing a bell at any time, he could make the pets slobber, even if there is no meat available.

It created a brain connection between the bell and the salivating activities, which is known as a programmed response.

You should employ a variety of "anchors" to stimulate and respond to yourself!

Anchoring oneself allows you to link your desired positive emotional reaction to a specific phrase or experience. When you actively tie a positive mood or image to a particular action, you will use this anchor whenever you feel weak, and your emotions will shift automatically.

1. Recognize what you expect to encounter (for starters, confidence, joy, peacefulness, etc.).

2. Choose a location for this anchor on your body, such as holding your earlobe, massaging your thumb, or gripping a fingertip.

3. Consider a time in the past when you were aware of the situation (e.g., confidence).

4. As you return to memory, pull/touch/shove the body part you've picked. The pleasure will increase as you replay the memories. Remove the pressure and continue to wear off as soon as the relationship circumstance improves.

5. This will establish stimulus-response neurology, which will activate the condition if the contact is rendered again. Only contact yourself in the same way again to feel the situation (e.g., esteem).

6. Consider another event in which you felt the condition, looked through and revisited it with your

eyes, and held the state in the same position as previously to improve the reaction. Each time you bring up a recall, the anchor becomes more powerful and will elicit a more robust response.

7. Using this method, you can change your mindset whenever you wish.

Pacing in the Future

Future pacing is a technique in which the practitioner asks the client to imagine how they may go about doing something in the future. While doing so, the NLP practitioner will keep track of the client's reactions.

The purpose of future pacing is to identify whether a change in progress was successful or not. This judgment will be made by the practitioner based on observations of body language. If the client's body language hasn't altered from previous attempts, the intervention was a flop. Another purpose of future pacing is to instil constructive change in the future. The client must take a more proactive approach to a problem, especially when the possible outcome is negative.

One of the primary advantages of using future pacing is that the customer will have experience with a specific situation before ever needing to be involved. They'll already have a positive reaction prepared. Although future pacing is dependent on vision, NLP practitioners believe that the mind cannot tell the difference between an actual scenario and one that has been clearly visualized. It may appear unusual at first, but it is straightforward to fool your mind into seeing things in a positive light.

The theory of future pacing is based on the idea that when you picture something positively, it serves as the ideal model of behaviour. Even a fictitious first experience can serve as a helpful starting point. In actuality, your behaviour simply accepts that original image, despite the fact that it was false. Subconsciously, your brain creates the change you wish to see when you face the stimulus again in the future—for real this time. Essentially, it is based on the notion that practice makes perfect.

Swish

This is an approach to NLP that redirects cognitive patterns so that the client no longer acts out an unpleasant behaviour but rather one that is desired. The way your subconscious tells you to behave is usually the most acceptable course of action. Whether or not it is a good deed is determined by a number of factors. Instead of slipping back into old negative habits, the client is encouraged to adopt new positive ones.

Swishing frequently necessitates the use of visual clues and acoustic elements. Unwanted behaviour resulting from these visuals is accompanied by auditory effects, facilitating the process of shifting from negative to good behaviour.

Finally, swishing is beneficial for a number of reasons. For many people, it helps alleviate feelings of humiliation and stress. Learning to swish might help you get rid of situations that are bringing you much pain. Of course, this strategy is best suited to dealing with minor concerns rather than major ones.

CHAPTER 4

NLP AND THE HUMAN BRAIN

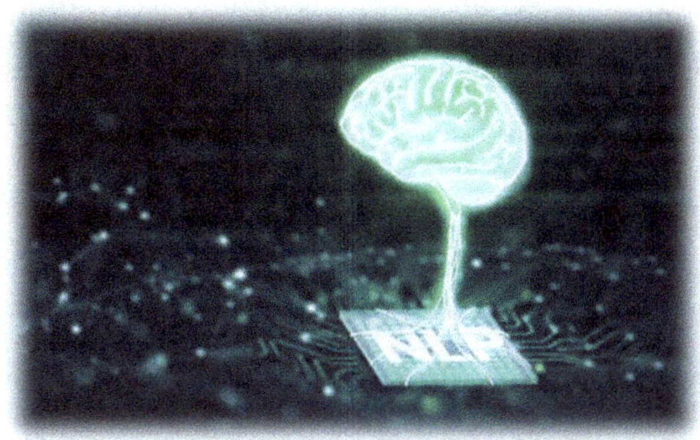

In its most basic form, NLP is a type of brain software that programs the way a human thinks. An NLP practitioner investigates the ways in which people think and seeks to remove all of the phobias, dogmas, and unfounded preconceptions that they have been dealing with up to this point. The technique regulates an individual's neurological thinking cycle.

NLP Is a Difficult Strategy

NLP may help with everything from enhancing family connections to advancing one's career! The programming method also aids in the recovery of persons suffering from trauma, phobias, and terminal illnesses. Inquire with others who have benefited from NLP approaches to demonstrate how effective the methodology is. NLP is credited to two great minds: Richard Bandler and John Grinder. This unique and powerful method was devised by two brilliant minds in the 1970s. Since then, the way this technology has been utilized to program behavioural habits, coordination, inspiration, and memory has substantially improved.

The method has evolved into one that is both intuitive and effective. NLP hypnosis remains a strange science for many people. Hypnosis is well ahead of simple NLP procedures. NLP hypnosis, often known as hypnotherapy, has grown in popularity since its introduction. The integration of NLP and NLP hypnosis is an intriguing subject. A person can become an expert in hypnosis with the help of neuro-linguistic training.

Mr Richard and Mr John pioneered a strategy that spans three major fields: neurology, languages, and computer science. The pair also collaborated on a book called "The Structure of Magic," which was published in 1975. They quickly began NLP classes to teach ordinary people how to benefit from NLP. Overall, NLP preparation aids in gaining a complete understanding of how a person works.

It aids in comprehending the impact of communication on the human psyche (both verbal and nonverbal). The process is essentially an in-depth language training of a person's mental mechanisms. It aids in the deciphering and replication of an individual's behavioural patterns. The strategy not only helps a person imitate the thinking of another person, but it also helps a person overcome self-limiting patterns. NLP (neuro-linguistic programming), often known as "modelling excellence," is a diagnostic approach. It is theoretically impossible to know. Only this can be understood experimentally.

Today, NLP is a thriving industry. NLP training practitioners, NLP coaching trainers, NLP courses, and NLP master mentors abound in the market. The technique's high-end benefits help draw folks to this fantastic mind tactic. Some institutes also provide free online NLP coaching. A person who is interested in such free NLP training programs might look for them in order to increase their confidence and capacity to interact.

As a Strategic Business Tool, NLP

I have been an NLP proponent and early adopter of NLP training in the company where I was the National Service and Training Manager from 1992. It was a location where forward-thinking, ambitious people thrived, and rapid growth was fostered. Those who first tried NLP to help them excel were the most ambitious. Initially, these were the selling managers looking for a competitive advantage in a fast-paced market. Marketing and marketing personnel promptly followed up with them.

Other accomplishments included a sales manager who landed a £60 million transaction with BT after learning how to build strong relationships with key influencers. It was a highly innovative and exciting time, and NLP was still relatively new in the UK. Today, NLP is taking centre stage as a standard answer to many competitive industrial concerns. Many successful practitioners have discovered that implementing NLP necessitates a high level of comprehension as well as a desire to break free from conventional thought.

Main Industries Where NLP Has a Significant Impact

Participation of the Leadership Workforce Recruiting Promotional Advertising Conferences and Workshops Preparation for Project Management Quality Team Work Reducing Stress Traditional wisdom is a significant impediment to NLP's effectiveness in the workplace, and my purpose here is to describe some of the difficulties encountered by persons who attempted to apply NLP in the workplace but failed.

NLP is an abbreviation for neuro-linguistic programming, which explains what happens in NLP training classes: you learn how to connect with the verbal and nonverbal language, and you may change or re-program your idea for better gain. You do acquire a good understanding of the mechanism of people-to-people contact, as well as some actual inspiration models. It was referred to as learning the art of subjective experience, which involved focusing on how a person thinks at any given time and responding to how you feel.

One of the most common misconceptions is that someone who has trained as a Practitioner can teach others what they have learned. When practising NLP, doctors are unlikely to be interested in the sophisticated methods that their NLP coaches employ to guarantee that learners are motivated and that practice sticks. Because NLP is such an engaging topic and people get so much from it, they appear to be passionate about teaching it to others. However, teaching NLP and explaining what you've learned to others is not the same thing.

Another mistake that businesses make is to use it to 'sheep-dip' people in NLP. The initial reaction to NLP may be similar to the Marmite approach—you either love it or despise it. As a result, sheep-dipping is not only ineffective but also needless, as you'll see later in this book.

An Effective Strategy

The format we've created over the years and recommend to our customers consists of five major stages:

1. Identify Your Target Audience

Determine where you want to incorporate an NLP strategy into your market first. If you start with a particular area, you will be able to quantify your growth in that field as a result of the effort you put in. In this location, the people are your audience, and your duty is to persuade them to participate in the show. Sales performance is one of the most straightforward applications to measure, and the results will be visible fast. Most salespeople are driven to learn anything that they believe would boost their sales volume.

Customer service, employee involvement, and teamwork may take a little longer to see the benefits, but the 'champion' approach generates a pull rather than a push for change. You create a Mexican wave-like chain reaction within the organization by educating those who are already eager to develop (champions or agents for advancement) and motivating them to demonstrate their positivism through skills. Signing up for the service requires no effort because more and more people volunteer. This is real commitment and empowerment in action, allowing the organization to support future initiatives for advancement.

2. Outcomes

The first question you've posted to your group is, 'What do you want NLP to do for you?'And this brings us to the critical question: what is the outcome? Choosing your products will help you focus on the application and measure the results, but these are only your outcomes. If you want to reach the audience, you must always provide precise comments. This is also a necessary component of any program that wishes to be implemented, although it is frequently overlooked. Learning inspiration necessitates the addition of specific interest to what you already know. Because that dimension was excluded from the front-end phase, it is reasonable to fail or attempt to comprehend or change policies.

3. Describe Your Current Experience

One of the basic tenets of NLP is that if people sense you respect them and are sincere in your intentions, they will allow you to influence them. They appreciate being guided with new ideas whenever it occurs. A typical example can be found in a sceptic response, where defending your concepts is the most common reaction.

This usually results in a tense territorial exchange. The NLP solution is to respect the cynic's point of view by saying something like, 'and you're right to be sceptical about new theories before you've thoroughly investigated them, or else we'll all accept it as true.' I'm always eager to collaborate with you because you've accomplished so much on your own.'

Pacing is all about establishing enough relationships to foster confidence in the relationship. Because people want to succeed, it makes it simpler to do everything else. This strategy is effective for 1:1 meetings, small groups, and large companies. The sole distinction between these is the time span in which you work for each. For example, in a 1:1 connection, the framing must incorporate the individual's expectations and preferences, and their input must determine the feedback. In a small community, your structure will be the same as in a 1:1; therefore, you'll need extra contact tactics to keep up with others. You will perform the same thing with an entire organization as you did with a small group, but you will utilize different communication tactics to involve a broader and more diverse set of people. You will very certainly frame your interaction with them in a far more comprehensive framework.

When it comes to pacing and leading large groups, consider a labour dispute to illustrate how a workforce's efforts are frequently overlooked by management. There would be fewer disagreements if executives chose to express gratitude for everyday triumphs rather than pushing for improvements. All too frequently, conflicts develop as a result of managers attempting to lead without first considering their past and current experiences.

4. Bring about a new experience

After a certain amount of pace, you can begin to lead. If you did a good job pacing, then teaching is a natural progression. The way in which you lead will be determined by your audience's motivating patterns. Whether you're leading a 1:1, a small team, or a large group, your readiness to listen and recognize trends of inspiration can teach you how to lead effectively. The more details you pay attention to, the faster you'll be able to move in.

If your motivations are authentic, truthful, and genuine, you will actively lead people. None of this can work if you have hidden motives or are insincere in any way. We have the ability to recognize deception. It is picked up unconsciously through tone of voice and body language.

Leading abilities are learned in an NLP Practitioner course, and they apply to leadership development just as much as they do to any other business sector. NLP is a resource for leaders who need to develop, engage, and motivate their people. We frequently find that managers who participate in our programs return to their firms and begin to exert more positive influence in a broader area of effect. They've acquired a really graceful and straightforward method of directing.

5. Maintain Your Integrity

Take note of hypotheses and generalizations. These are some of the disadvantages of current exercises, workshops, and conferences. A concept is only valuable if it can be implemented. Typically, executing a new principle entails a further action that comes with experience - otherwise, the old habits persist. Many people can regurgitate theories but are unable to act on them.

One of the most common questions we get at the beginning of our NLP classes is, "Should an individual do x in this situation?" In such a case, the questioner attempts to foresee everyone. Of course, this is rubbish. Our typical response to the inquiry is, 'Who?' As I previously stated, NLP is the study of subjective experience, thus unlike conventional psychology, we do not attempt to create 'norms' because they do not serve us. At the time, we wish to interact in order to interpret the scenario. Our communications will be more realistic and efficient as a result.

Another learning challenge is the conjecture. Some people will play it out in their heads as they listen to a teacher discuss a tactic or situation, asking themselves, "How does that work?" They accomplish this by putting themselves in the picture and imagining how it will play out for them. This is OK if you only remember the process, but some people take it a step farther and anticipate a horrible outcome to the process. This leads people to think, 'this wouldn't work for me,' and voila, a barrier to learning is created. Only by putting something into practice and being honest about the results can you actually learn how it will succeed—not just in your head.

These are only a few of the more significant barriers to learning new skills. There are several alternatives that traditional trainers are unlikely to consider. NLP trainers are pretty competent at spotting many of these cognitive difficulties and adapting their training methods to assist people in overcoming them and continuing to learn. If there is one thing that NLP gives anyone, it is the ability to learn more intelligently and efficiently.

CHAPTER 5
TIPS FOR APPLYING NLP

Using NLP may be a new and unfamiliar experience for you at first, but there are several methods you can take to make NLP easier to understand. NLP will change the way you think, but it will not happen immediately. You will need to devote some time to learning how to modify your way of thinking.

Tip 1: The Why Question

'Why?' is a question that many people can't help but ask, and it will ultimately lead nowhere because you won't always be able to find out why things happen. Sometimes things just happen for the sake of happening. A more efficient query would be to figure out how to solve the problem at hand.

Tip 2: Your behaviour is almost never incorrect.

However, you can engage in that conduct and, in some cases, in an inappropriate setting. For example, if you are afraid of being around sharp items because of anything that happened in your past, that is a totally understandable concern. However, it will not be acceptable if you are afraid in a restaurant even when you are not using a sharp object, but other people are. Your anxieties can overwhelm you, but it is up to you to determine whether to let them come through and when to try to work through them.

Tip 3: Manage Your Emotions

The feelings you experience are the result of something that occurs in your brain. You will not share feelings simply because you are thinking about them. Most emotions come to the surface when you engage in an activity that triggers them. So, instead of concentrating on those feelings, why not try something new? If you find yourself in the same scenario again, try something different to see if you can obtain a different result.

Tip 4: Your Point of View

Looking at all the terrible in the world will lead you to find something to be concerned about or disturbed about. There is so much awful in the world that you will be able to locate it even if you don't try very hard. All you have to do is glance at the news to find something wrong with the world. So, begin to train yourself to search for the good in life. It may be more difficult to find, but it will assist with your depression because you will not have to focus on all the negative aspects of life; instead, you will focus on the positive aspects of life.

Tip 5: Accepting Compliments

Compliments can be challenging to accept at times, but refusing to accept them will make you wonder if you feel good about yourself. Because of your existing ideas, you may be tempted to question and mistrust every time someone says something pleasant to you. However, you will discover that compliments will assist you in dealing with your despair. Having other people realize what you've done might increase your self-esteem. So, if you don't think you deserve to be complimented, either accomplish something worth being approved on or adjust your beliefs so that you can accept praise. Compliments aren't always awful! They are a human's way of stating that they have noticed and appreciate what has been done.

Tip 6: Speaking to Yourself

It may be difficult for you to accept, but you will be talking to yourself every day in your thoughts. Most of the time, the voice you hear in your brain will be different from the voice you use when speaking to other people. If you find it challenging to communicate to yourself because your inner voice is not supportive, it is time to adjust your inner voice. This will assist a lot with depression because you will be shifting your perspective on yourself. If you can't accept yourself for who you are, how can you expect others to?

Tip 7: When Issues Arise

Problems that develop in your life may appear to be interminable. However, instead of viewing the challenges that life throws at you as if they will never stop, consider them to be opportunities for you to transform your life. All you have to do is use your imagination to look at how the problem arises and realize that, while it may put you back, it may also propel you forward so that you can constructively manage your depression.

Tip 8: It Doesn't Matter What Has Happened in the past.

You will not be able to change it, no matter how badly you want to. It also doesn't matter what emotions you felt at the time because they are gone. The past is the past, and you will not return to it. The only way to make a difference in the future is to let go and keep moving forward. Learn from your mistakes and keep moving forward. If you don't learn from your mistakes, you'll make them again, and even if the past is gone, it will keep repeating itself until you finally understand and stop making the same mistakes.

Tip 9: Remember to Breathe

Inhale from the pit of your stomach for the most pleasing results. This will not only help to calm your anxieties, but it will also help to control your physiology. Remaining calm will be the best technique for you to stay calm in instances where your tension is high. The more you manage your breathing, the more likely you are to remain calm and make the right option while reacting to something someone has said or done.

CHAPTER 6
PRESUPPOSITIONS IN NLP

When we discuss the foundations of NLP or the classics of NLP, we are also debating presuppositions. NLP, you see, isn't based on many theories. It is based on what works in practice. "If it works, it's NLP," Bandler and Grinder were famous for saying. What we're doing here is looking for folks who have achieved the required results and then determining whether or not what they did to achieve that result was successful.

This is one of the reasons it is difficult to put to the academic test in peer-reviewed journals. Peer-reviewed research examines theories and test hypotheses, yet there are no hypotheses in NLP. We have the experiences of others who have gone before us, which is incredibly practical.

Replicating Successful Patterns

The founders of NLP were ecstatic to be able to repeat the results of Virginia Satir, medical hypnotherapist Milton Erickson, psychologist and psychotherapist Fritz Perls, and others they studied. And they were eager to disseminate the results without paying any thought to the philosophical underpinnings. What has happened in the last forty or fifty years, which we do not spend much time discussing in NLP classes, is that we have learned the psychobiology of behavioural and emotional responses.

The work of Bruce Lipton and others who have written on the subject, both in academia and popular psychology, has helped us grasp the mind/body relationship. And we now hold the relevance of our brain, the literal brain, in developing the ability to access and repeat the success patterns revealed and identified via NLP.

I enjoy writing about NLP in the context of acceptance and commitment therapy and mindfulness-based stress reduction. We already know that the mind is not wired to remain in the current moment. Because of evolutionary biology, our minds seek the past to predict the future. And it is always reading history to determine the future. This is how the mind works, but we can invent, practice, and use approaches like mindfulness-based stress reduction to teach people to do something the brain is not naturally predisposed to do: live entirely in the present moment.

As a result, people are better able to deal with stress. They make better decisions, have better relationships, and are more likely to be able to live out their intents and dreams.

Primary Representational Systems (PRS)

The primary representational systems were the focus of classic NLP. Consider this in terms of the five senses: olfactory, taste, gustatory, smell, and so on. The majority of people do not learn through olfactory or gustatory means. They are typically known by auditory, visual, or tactile means. Tactile, feeling, and touching are all examples of kinesthetic. These five senses are how we see our surroundings. And the importance of defining a person's primary representational system was realized by the early writers in NLP. Do they act as auditory learners and experiencers? Are they acting as visual learners and observers? Do they have a tactile sense of the world around them?

How do you tell if you are auditory, visual, or kinesthetic, or if the person with whom you are working is auditory, visual, or kinesthetic? I placed it in the context of modern times with IKEA furnishings.

How might constructing IKEA furniture assist us in determining what representational system we have?

The auditory learner interacts with the world by hearing and saying things. They read the directions because they have physically "heard" them in their minds.

The visual experience looks at the picture on the box, examines all of the components, and attempts to build what they perceive.

The kinesthetic experiencer picks up the pieces, touches them, and feels both the painted and unfinished sides. They bring them together. They can tell which bits are heavier, more prominent, or smaller. And they construct it by feeling it.

The manner in which you construct IKEA furniture can indicate your central representational system. It is critical that we have a basic representative system. Our customers are experiencing their difficulties through auditory means, whether it is through self-talk or messages pushed by others. They are viewing their future in a visual way, either adversely or optimistically. Or they are feeling the weight of their emotions or the lightness and strength of victory. The early NLP practitioners concentrated on assessing the client's primary representational system and then encouraging us to be congruent so that we could work within the skill sets they had to help them attain their full potential.

The issue with that notion is that it is pretty limited. It is constricting since our clients will return to the real world. The real world, on the other hand, is auditory. It is kinesthetic in nature. It is visible. It has an olfactory component. It's delicious. There are a variety of sensory sensations. When I have a client who has good optical acuity but poor kinesthetic acuity, I work with them to improve their kinesthetic sensitivity. When my clients have a low level of auditory sense and a high level of kinesthetic insight, rather than simply trying to master kinesthetic awareness, I help them learn how to increase their auditory acuity so that they can operate holistically in the world, and the easiest way to engage people is to establish rapport with them. And NLP training is always centred on developing skills and building rapport.

Proxemics

Proxemics simply refers to attending to or being with someone and the effect that has on them. We have a psycho-physiological reaction to the presence of other people. This explains how I can improve my rapport-building abilities by better understanding proxemics and my interpersonal relationships. These ideas were viable forty or fifty years ago, but they are still possible now.

How do we position ourselves with clients in the office? As a hypnotherapist and life coach, I frequently deliver my pre-talk at my front table. Because there is some space between them and me, my client feels comfortable. When my client is satisfied, and rapport is established, we proceed to the hypnotic furniture, my client to the recliner, and I to my chair—near them, closer to them, sharing trance experiences.

I don't consider myself to be a hypnotist, a therapist, or a coach to anyone. I see myself as sharing a trance with them, sharing expertise with them, or sharing the resources that have helped me transform, and I support the people I deal with transform so that they can reap the advantages of others who have gone before them.

Success Patterns

We discuss patterns reproducing success in conventional NLP.

This is at the heart of life coaching: assisting people in reaching their highest degree of potential. Patterns can be replicated. Patterns of success can help me in conquering challenging emotions, becoming motivated, and developing a set of resource states that are important to me. All of these are examples of NLP patterns. The Swish Pattern and the Six-Step Reframe are two famous patterns you may have heard of. All of these are basic NLP patterns, but the question is, what new ways can we create? And can we train them for different professions?

In the context of sales, we can look at examples of outstanding salespeople, such as Zig Ziglar. We can make a pattern out of these people because they were not considered in early NLP. However, if one wishes to be a successful salesperson, we must examine modern exemplars in this or any other business and question whether these stages to success can be boiled down into a formula or a pattern, taught to others, and then repeated. Almost always, the answer is yes.

Levels of Neurology

The neurological levels are concerned with the who, what, when, and how. These are well-known NLP ideas, as are language patterns. However, language evolves. The identical terminology we use today did not exist forty or fifty years ago. It is estimated that in fifty years, 20% of the common language, or everyday language used by individuals, will have changed from what it was in previous years. What evidence do we have that this is correct? Read a vintage book. The language is out of date. Furthermore, the language patterns examined in early NLP and still taught in many classes are not necessarily the language patterns that people use today.

CHAPTER 7
COMMUNICATION AND NLP

The human mind has always been a mysterious realm that not even neuroscience, with all of its breakthroughs, has been able to comprehend fully. Each person's subjectivity, belief system, conventions, habits, and so on are all recorded directly in mind. We cannot interpret these processes individually because they are so intricate. Do you want to know where to start when it comes to unravelling the enigma of the mind?

The answer is closer than you think: language and communication lead to mental territory. It's no coincidence that philosophers like Martin Heidegger have remarked that "language is the house of existence." Communication action through Neurolinguistic Programming (NLP), developed in the mid-1970s by psychotherapist and computer scientist Richard Bandler and linguist John Grinder, has brought better practicality in this aspect.

NLP communication is one of the most successful techniques for reshaping people's subjectivities at all levels. On the one hand, neurolinguistics, which captures brain activity from language, and communication in all its forms (verbal and nonverbal), make it a handy instrument. As a result, NLP and communication are inextricably intertwined. It is about programming, but it also gives you formal structures for changing your belief systems. In this sense, if you are stuck at work or in a love relationship, communicating with NLP can assist you to redirect the attitudes you face in your life and therefore achieve the success you have always desired.

It functions and successfully stimulates communicative action as a learning approach for the development of human skills because of NLP. In other words, NLP communication pushes you closer and closer not only to understanding but also to programming your mind for successful skill development.

What Exactly Is NLP Communication?

Neurolinguistic Programming is a technique for gaining access to a person's mental content. NLP provides you with learning models for optimizing belief systems. In the first instance, she is born as a therapeutic method. However, its use is now much broader: organizations, institutions, and coaching, in general, are becoming increasingly interested in this strategy.

Believe it or not, success is right around the corner; you will notice that your communication and speech with neurolinguistics programming, as well as all elements of your life, will shift towards healing, peace, and the optimum use of your mind. Remember that your brain works by repetition or by what you are most comfortable with.

As a result, in whatever situation, your mind takes the same path. Neurolinguistics programs, on the other hand, are learning approaches that improve your ability to respond to specific situations. If you are still not convinced, we assure you that with NLP, successful communication, mental scheme programming, speech development, confidence, performance, self-esteem, proactivity, and so on.

NLP induces a shift in your belief system. By using NLP to change your beliefs, you may convince yourself of your success and eliminate negative self-concepts. This is established by Richard Bandler, co-creator of NLP communication, when he says, "The key to success is beliefs." "I modelled many successful persons," says Richard Bandler in an interview with Coaching Portal in 2006. This is how NLP communication may mould your mind for success in any aspect of your life.

Laws of NLP Communication

The NLP and communication model are pragmatic theory that relies on modelling behaviours to improve your quality of life. The laws or parameters of NLP communication can be broken down into three major categories:

It is impossible to avoid communication. The most critical NLP tool in interpersonal communication, responsible for connecting successful behaviours to your own subjective experiences.

Move your body and let it speak for you! When practising NLP communication, you must be alert and anticipate any nonverbal language, or body language, reaction. Addressing these nonverbal signs of language is critical to improving your cognitive programming.

If what you've been doing hasn't been providing you with the happiness you require, it's time to try something new. It impacts more than you realize in NLP communication to modify the mindset with which you communicate. You must engage in everyday exercises such as talking about the good, reacting physically in a caring manner, and believing that success is attainable in any personal or professional activity you undertake.

Communication Channels for NLP

In this technology age, there are numerous routes through which communication and NLP can be communicated to people of all types, including you and me. Similarly, the breadth of this approach is pretty broad, and the most convenient way to access its teachings is via the internet, via specific web portals. However, because modelling your mind is a time-consuming process that necessitates patience and competent professors, we propose that you visit reputable websites such as the Teleseminar NLP High School.

Dr Edmundo Velasco (Physician by profession and specialized in Gestalt psychotherapy) founded the NLP Higher School in Mexico after working directly with John Grinder, co-founder of NLP communication. This school's mission is to include more and more people who are eager to work on their emotional and productive lives through NLP and effective communication lessons.

This programming school is one of the most prestigious in the entire Spanish-speaking region, with roots in the fundamental concepts of NLP communication. It provides a wide range of courses, from face-to-face classes taught by Dr Velasco himself to online workshops, where you can obtain a certificate as a Facilitator of change processes with NLP after participating in the transformation of your life aimed at success (if you are one of those who are emerging as leaders), and thus master the communication with NLP and become a positive influence for everyone around you.

Communication Styles in NLP

People are language beings. As a result, your need to express yourself and communicate is fundamental. The integration of language as spoken or written word and language not spoken but expressed through our body, through gestures, expressions, postures, and so on, is the basis for the creation or modification of mental structures and belief systems, according to neuro-linguistic communication and programming. As a result, NLP employs verbal, nonverbal, and visual language as resources to effect effective mental change in people.

Verbal Communication Using NLP

It is, by definition, the sort of communication that takes place through the use of spoken language. According to neurolinguistics, this style of communication allows us to receive an entire world of symbols and meanings from the outside world and then translate them, in the letter, into the spoken word. When you use NLP to access hand communication, you sharpen your brain receptors, allowing you to employ verbal communication more efficiently and consistently as needed.

Nonverbal Communication (NLP)

When you hear that there is nonverbal communication neurolinguistics programming within the NLP approach, it is not unusual or difficult to access resources. Nonverbal communication, on the other hand, is the vast universe of an unspoken language, that is, the body language and symbolic systems via which it acts, namely:

- Time management is a chromonema.
- The pimping is a spatial arrangement of bodies.
- Diacritics are the symbols that govern the spatial structure of items and colours.
- The paralinguistic: vocal tones
- Gestures, postures, motions, and reactions of the body are all examples of kinesics.

Visual Communication Using NLP

Although both verbal and nonverbal communication is essential in the proper management of NLP communication as a method of self-improvement, it is worth highlighting visual communication as the most popular form of communication in our day, especially with the introduction of new technological devices and the widespread use of social networks. It is true that the influence of a person, piece of information, or event is felt first and foremost through sight. That is why NLP appropriates this resource, with the goal of channelling the way you seem in front of others and making the best impression possible.

These sorts of NLP communication create a set of applications that you can use on a daily basis to help you measure your personality and achieve the performance and success you require in your life.

Language of the Body

What do we convey, and how do we transmit it?

Understanding body language is essential and can save us in a variety of situations. Let's look into it.

What Is the Difference Between Informing and Communicating?

We inform when we share information, and we don't need or care about what comes after that. I have told you, and that is sufficient for me. I want you to take this information and apply it to what you believe is best for you.

However, communicating is anotherstory.

We communicate because we want something in return, even if it is only an answer. We share because we have a goal to achieve, whatever that goal may be.

Every communication has worth; even when we don't speak, we communicate. Looks, postures, and facial expressions all provide information.

That nonverbal component of communication, for the most part, is because the messages of the body transmit the most.

How many times has someone told you something and, despite the fact that his words were extra-convincing and his tone of voice was the most acceptable, a small voice within warned you that there was something that didn't convince you?

Recognize Body Language

Our ability to read body language and its signals assists us in gaining a better understanding of what individuals are trying to express.

People can say yes and then move their heads to signify no.

Who says he's overjoyed to see you and gradually draws his body back?

Who knows how bored he was at the party and how quickly he licked his lips?

It's interesting to see how much our bodies speak in order to get a sense of what those unconscious movements that individuals make while talking to us indicate.

Body language messages can be divided into three macro-categories:

1.   Satisfaction messages
2.   Squander messages
3.   Discharges of tension

Body Language Messages of Satisfaction

These are the subliminal messages that our interlocutor's body conveys without their conscious awareness. They express their admiration for what we are saying or doing at the time.

Here are several examples:

•   Linguine, you're nodding and saying yes with your head.

•   Caressing analogue kiss (hair, body)

•   Approaches with the entire body Arms and legs not crossed Smiling

•   Body Language Rejection Messages

If the approval messages show that what is going on between us pleases our interlocutor,

The rejection messages show the opposite.

Here are several examples:

- You should shake your head.

- Cross your legs and arms.

- The body is removed.

- Position yourself to the side.

Tension Discharges in Body Language

These body cues indicate that what we are saying or doing is causing tension in our interlocutor, an accumulation of energy that has to be released. Here are several examples:

- Itching

- sighs

- Fingers tapping

- Consume your nails

- Move the legs with trepidation to be

- blushing

- Swallow/scrape throat

They must be contextualized: crossing one's legs does not imply that the individual is conveying to us that he disagrees with what we are saying.

Perhaps, but most emphatically not.

If there are multiple messages of the same type, the news that arrives will be the correct one.

Have fun seeing which of these few body language signs people who will engage with you tomorrow utilize!

CHAPTER 8
NLP IN BUSINESS

Companies all around the world have begun to adopt NLP methodologies because they offer enormous benefits that can propel a company to the next level. Using NLP approaches nearly guarantees the most basic degree of income improvements. As a result, peer-to-peer communication will vastly improve. NLP is just what the business world needs.

Neuro-linguistic programming has various business applications. Motivation pattern management, cognitive change technology, conflict resolution, training and coaching, guidance, learning, and teaching are examples of these. All of these dimensions must deal with sentiments at some point, and once dealt with, these feelings are highly beneficial.

When people use NLP methods in any industry, it may make a massive difference because it is possible to modify behaviour in such a way that everyone is striving towards it with a successful NLP practice.

Any firm that wants to prosper should focus on four concepts:

Work to Get Results

Positive usage of NLP necessitates the establishment of objectives and the pursuit of those objectives. In general, this method refers to a business setting. When you understand what your intended purpose is, your mind is better prepared to manage the steps that will be performed to help you accomplish that outcome. The idea is to be aware of your actions, and NLP excels at this.

Being aware might help your organization stand out from the crowd in the business world. Instead of focusing on what they want, NLP-free businesses may focus on what they don't want. Working with a negative attitude will still attract a negative attitude; in other words, negative attitudes will result in unfavourable outcomes. NLP emphasizes the importance of focusing on the product and staying focused on it. It also preaches positivism and demonstrates that even destructive deeds can have great intentions.

These outcomes must be expressed positively in order to be realized. It ensures that they are always focused on the "bright side" rather than tasks that cannot be completed. Expected results must be sensory-specifically tested and observable to confirm that they are realistic. The suggestion here is that there should be some proof that the outcome was met. To be sensory-specific, you must be able to convey yourself through language and feelings when you achieve your goal.

When working toward a goal, it must be launched and sustained by one guy. This individual must be in charge of the outcome from start to finish so that activities can be regulated and adjusted as needed. The idea here is that an individual in the organization can use NLP to cause a wave of positive change through their actions. It also allows you to hold people accountable for their conduct – or you get a bonus.

Every action elicits an equal or positive reaction. You are attentive to your activities and their potential consequences by practising NLP to guarantee that no harm is done to you or others. You can also model positive behaviour so that when others emulate what they see in you, you will only receive positive feedback.

Understand and Be Conscious of Your Senses

You will be able to read other people easily once you have learned how to apply NLP. It comprises any nonverbal signs people employ when interacting with you, whether consciously or unintentionally. You must sharpen your senses as you become more aware of them.

Changes in skin colour (blushing or pale), increased or decreased breathing rates, and noticeable muscle-flexing Recognizing these shifts can be helpful when dealing with a client since it allows the NLP practitioner to determine what kind of impact they have on other people.

This recognition will also assist the NLP therapist in quitting when the other person has attained their intended result.

Assume you work in the sales department of a bustling clothes store. When a customer walks in, you notice that they have broken out in a cold sweat, are out of breath, and constantly staring at their watch even before they begin buying.

If you used NLP approaches, you might discover that the client is in a rush and wants to be served fast in order to make their next appointment. As a result, you may change the amount of service you provide accordingly.

Change Your Behavior to Ensure a Successful Outcome

It is directly related to the first premise and delves into the essence of NLP, which is behavioural transformation. In a business setting, you must be adaptable enough to shift gears when the expected response does not materialize.

This strategy is only effective if you keep your end objective in mind at all times, primarily if you use the modelling authority and have a clear picture of the steps you need to do to get there.

As explained in the second principle, use your ability to measure the response. If you get the intended result, you must stick to your predetermined plan of action. However, if you do not achieve the desired effect, you should try a different strategy.

Spending time studying and monitoring your activities can potentially spare you stress and frustration if you are cognizant of your sentiments and how you can cope with them.

Take Initiative

It is necessary for NLP to be actively involved in decision-making at this time. It is pointless to spend time learning all of the NLP techniques if you do not put your reading skills to the test.

The important thing is to work to modify behaviours; it is critical to act in the present. Changing and improving behaviour gets more manageable when one is present. Companies that send their employees to NLP skills training, particularly practitioner skills, frequently send only their leadership team with the expectation that they will learn a new skill that will then be passed down to the rest of the group.

NLP is not a resource that should be restricted to a company's leadership. Instead, it is a piece of software that everyone in the company should be familiar with in order to ensure that the corporate goals are met. Employees can employ NLP techniques to produce better results or connect more effectively with consumers.

When using NLP tools to deal with customers or connect internally, the effect is often quite clear–a percentage increase in consumer purchases or employee productivity.

When an employee is trained to learn NLP skills at any point, they are highly motivated, which usually results in increased output. NLP should teach any worker how to create, understand, and apply anything that can be done on a mental map.

The preceding points highlight the most common business challenges. The main challenge is effective communication. What happens in a company and what happens to customers are both covered by communication?

NLP is helpful in practically every aspect of a business, and it benefits both employers and employees. NLP strategies and activities can be used by employees in an organization to:

• Set specific, measurable goals and work to attain them.

• Increase your confidence in your ability to work and perform better all of the time.

• Boost their morale and keep them motivated throughout the organization.

• Recognize some of the obstacles that prevent people from accomplishing their professional goals.

• Management will also apply NLP talents in a variety of areas, such as developing strong and meaningful connections with other people in business, employees, suppliers, customers, and anybody else who is essential to the company.

During performance-improvement discussions, they end up establishing the company's best customer service base to meet all of its customers' needs. Nonetheless, diversity may be a requirement that customers require when resolving disputes and issues between the company and its employees, the business and its clients, and the business and other businesses.

NLP talents can assist in determining how the organization can establish teams that function even better and consistently produce exceptional results. In general, NLP techniques can be used to boost business sales.

Using NLP to Increase Sales

Every company, big or small, wants to increase sales. Businesspeople will go to almost any length to increase their sales volume, as this is what determines how well a company is doing. Today, NLP is used by salespeople, sales managers, business people, and entrepreneurs to enhance their sales volumes. Even a successful firm or a skilled salesperson will benefit from some pointers to help them stay on top of their game when it comes to earning more money.

Because salespeople and their consumers have various interactions, NLP can be really beneficial. Neuro-linguistic programming is a set of ideas and abilities that combine people's brains, bodies, and feelings to allow them to communicate effectively with others. If you work in sales, these are the talents and methods that will help you advance your career.

Everyone has a preferred language in which they prefer to talk or listen. You must understand and use the language that others prefer in order to connect with your customers. Listen carefully when your consumers speak and determine whether they want to utilize visual or auditory words, then employ the language they want to sell in.

Your consumers' purchasing strategy must match your sales plan. When visual noises are more appealing to a possible buyer, you will need to use sound to capture his attention. Carry samples to attract the attention of customers who prefer to see them before they buy.

CHAPTER 9
NLP IN RELATIONSHIPS

In this section, we will learn how NLP can benefit healthy relationships. We shall discover the foundations and pillars of unique and fulfilling relationships. We will look at tactics that can help us strengthen relationships as well as those that can help us develop healthy ones. We will discuss the benefits or relevance of our mental health and readiness before entering any partnership or relationship, as well as the possible results of having or not having these characteristics.

Once you've decided what you want, it's time to get into a relationship and address your deciding reasons. You can now begin to consider the possibility of meeting the right person. This is where rapport comes into play.

What exactly is rapport? It is your similarity and likeness to someone with whom you want to be in a relationship. It's also the beginning of a relationship with that person. Many individual criteria can be utilized to determine compatibility with rapport. Personality types, values, beliefs, culture, political ideologies, interests, religious beliefs, and so on are examples of these. Of course, physical parameters such as gender and body type must be taken into account. Some traits, however, cannot be overemphasized because they will imitate the other and produce a loss of rapport.

The initial rapport, the reasons for your attraction to your partner, and their attraction to you must remain at the forefront of each partner's consciousness throughout the relationship. It is all too often for people to approach partnerships with guns blazing, implying that they will be the perfect mate, only to relax and adapt once the connection is established. One or both partners will try every conceivable strategy to persuade the other to join into a relationship. The other person believes that once they are in that relationship, they can initially tone down what they were doing. It is one of the most common causes for relationships to end.

Keep in mind that the reasons someone falls in love with you are the same reasons they will want to stay with you. They have no incentive to stay with you if the reasons for their attraction are removed. Children born from relationships are frequently touted as fresh reasons, but this does not work. It causes the collaboration to evolve into a business connection. There will be no genuine emotional connection in the relationship, and even if the couple stays together, they will be deprived of the comforts and fulfilment of their wants.

You've identified what you want, ensured that the timing is ideal, and met that special someone. So, what are you going to do now? You must verify that your significant other has the same feelings about you. A person might see that they are loved by others in a variety of ways. These ways should be identified at the start of the relationship. Some tactics include what the other person buys and where they go to you. There are other factors to consider, such as how they touch you, the looks they give you, or what they say. Identification of these is critical since they can predict the persistence of love during the relationship.

The most accessible approach to discover how to assure your mate best that you love them is to do what they do for you. For example, if your spouse occasionally wraps her arm around you to assure you of her love and affection, you can trust that if you do the same, she will believe that you love and appreciate her. We don't do things to or for others that we wouldn't want to be done to us, especially those we care about the most. Although this is obvious, it is also a fantastic way to measure or determine how your significant other feels about you. As the relationship develops, this will become more natural and require less deliberate effort. Make sure that these things do not come to an end just because the relationship is no longer new.

NLP has developed a few ways for determining regions of conflict in relationships. NLP approaches are used to strategize areas like attraction, love, and desire. First and foremost, you must become acquainted with your spouse. It means you should be aware of the subtle gestures and tones of voice your spouse will exhibit depending on how they are feeling. Understand your partner's worries and desires. Simply learning from your partner will provide you with ideas on how to carry out these tasks. Make sure that you never use this knowledge to manipulate others. When there is manipulation in a relationship, there is no beneficial conclusion.

Remove yourself from your partner's company for a short period of time to verify that they are in love with you and desire you. That doesn't mean you should inform your wife you're heading to the shop for a lottery ticket and won't be back for a week. In a short period of time, absence can indicate a lack of want. Absence, like the cliché, makes the heart grow fonder; this is based on the same idea. Please don't overdo it with these kinds of methods. Here's some guidance. If you are an insecure person who needs regular approval and confirmation that you are loved, you should address this issue before engaging in a meaningful relationship. You will not be a suitable mate if you do not. If your flaw does not lead to the end of the relationship, it may lead to it becoming a codependent partnership or, at the very least, a very toxic relationship. Again, before going that further step, you must first ensure that you are the proper candidate for entering into a relationship.

When it comes to relationships, you are not simply selling yourself to another person, and then the job is done. It is an ongoing process that will never end. Never, ever believe that you have your partner and that you aren't going anywhere, no matter what you do or don't do. You should consistently market yourself, your worth, your compassion, and your desire for your partner.

Consider this: you meet someone at the beach or any other location you can think of. You're both in the same place at the same time. You may have everything in common as well. However, you and the other individual travelled separate routes to that location and encountered various conditions along the way. Despite the fact that you both find yourself at the exact location and with the same traits, you follow different roads to get there. It implies that you are unlikely to react or respond to every incident in the same way and that those occurrences may take you in opposite ways.

Another way to look at it is that you may both be fans of the same sports team. The distinction is why every one of you has a different perspective of that team. One of you may have graduated from that university, while the other simply chose the champions from the previous season. It is likely that the school's alumni are less inclined to determine that they no longer support that team. Regardless of the conceivable outcomes, the conclusion stays the same.

What exactly does this mean? Are we all at the mercy of life, prone to emotional pain at the drop of a hat? No, not exactly. We may not be able to change the scenario that has brought us here, but we can learn why. First and foremost, don't give up. Do whatever you can to help both you and your spouse get through the bad patch in your relationship, and you might find that you were able to beat the odds and stay together.

Let's take a closer look at what it means to have chosen distinct paths. The circumstances that were just stated were merely metaphors. The location is not a physical site but rather a unique state of mind and life condition. Whatever commonality you and your partner may or may not have, you will both respond and react differently to situations. One of you might be able to brush things off, such as a tragic occurrence, but the other cannot.

Consider this: both you and your wife are religious. It is one of the significant similarities you discovered in yourself that led to your partnership. Then, later in life, your wife either experiences a tragic event or meets an influential person, both of which cause a radical shift in her religious ideas. What was once the fundamental glue that held you together has deteriorated to the point where it is no longer present. Not only does she no longer agree with your religious convictions, but her newest opinions contradict yours. What should you do in this situation? You both are adamant about your personal convictions and are unwilling to compromise. Both accuse the other of naiveté. You're not bad people, but you're not having the same connection you used to.

You both entered the relationship after taking the necessary steps and exercising due to prudence in selecting the other as a mate. Even if this was completed, life was unconcerned. Circumstances caused you and your partner's beliefs to diverge, and you're both far too committed to your different ideas to compromise them. As a result, you are constantly at odds, and the negativity in your relationship grows stronger by the day. It will eventually develop into resentment and maybe hatred. You've taken the required efforts to try to save the relationship, but it's been futile. So, as a final resort, you decide to split up. It happens on a daily basis.

We have lessons learned and unique ways of dealing with specific difficulties based on these lessons, just as the baggage we carry from previous terrible relationships. The best thing to do is to be aware of what is going on and how things are progressing, as this will give you a fair sense of what is to come.

To summarize this advice, NLP is necessary and reasonable in the relationship. It's not just at the start of the union but all the way through. You must first understand yourself, and then, with the help of NLP, you may learn about your relationship. Knowing your partner can be quite beneficial in maintaining a good and long-lasting relationship. Furthermore, the relationship will be far more fulfilling for both parties. Remember that severe and intimate relationships are helpful in many aspects of life, not only the partnership. It's good for you as a couple, as individuals, and as members of society.

CONCLUSION

Whether you want to use NLP or manipulation, read body language, or use hypnosis to enhance yourself or influence others, there is one trait that will increase your chances of success with all four methods: confidence. It's simple: if you don't believe in yourself, why should anyone else base their beliefs on you? Maintain your confidence by referring to the postural advice and methods in this book.

You're probably not sure where to begin in your effort to shield oneself against dark psychology. Given the breadth of this book's content, you must allow yourself enough time to study the defence measures one by one. An in-depth understanding of NLP would be a fantastic starting point. As soon as you can read people's minds using NLP, you will be well on your way to protecting yourself and everyone in your family from manipulation.

Anyone can learn how to use NLP. It is not a secret reserved for a select few.

When you are ready to study a little bit more about NLP, incredibly dark NLP, use this guidebook to ensure that you get started on the proper course.

Keep in mind that these procedures are not scientifically established but have been tested and developed over time based on experience and outcomes.

Reading this book does not preclude you from reading another book about NLP Dark Psychology; knowledge is never enough, thus increasing your knowledge is always the most significant thing to do.

You should get started now that you've read the book and understand everything. Mind control, manipulation, and persuasive methods are the ultimate deals to employ in your daily life; it does not have to be this way.

To you, it appears to be an immoral act. Learning how to control and persuade people teaches you how to govern the mental processes of others or become a manipulator yourself.

Even if you don't wish to be a manipulator or persuader, you've learned about the morality and immorality of dark psychology principles like mind control, manipulation, and persuasion. If the strategies sound helpful to you, you can use them in advertising, politics, the media, religion, or even at home and school.

Each person has a distinct personality and behaviour, which limits how well each NLP technique can operate for them.

When you have control over the tactics, you may choose them intelligently based on where, when, and for whom they are used, rather than allowing them to dictate your mind and cognitive process. Persuasion, bargaining, or manipulation cannot be achieved through precisely defined stages or techniques. Instead, it may behave differently depending on a variety of factors such as behavioural patterns, attitudes, circumstances, and personalities. As a result, it is entirely up to you to develop a recipe for NLP approaches that will work successfully for you.

www.ingramcontent.com/pod-product-compliance
Lightning Source LLC
LaVergne TN
LVHW020608200726
843509LV00001B/26